CRISIS MANAGEMENT

A Team Approach

Robert F. Littlejohn

AMA Management Briefing

AMA MEMBERSHIP PUBLICATIONS DIVISION
AMERICAN MANAGEMENT ASSOCIATIONS

Library of Congress Cataloging in Publication Data

Littlejohn, Robert F., 1941-
    Crisis management

    (AMA management briefing)
    1. Crisis management. I. Title. II. Series.
    HD49.L57   1983   658.4   83-12282
    ISBN 0-8144-2295-0

This Management Briefing has been distributed to all members enrolled in the General Management and Public Management Divisions of the American Management Associations. Copies may be purchased at the following single-copy rates: AMA members, $7.50. Nonmembers, $10.00. Students, $3.75 (upon presentation of a college/university identification card at an AMA bookstore). Faculty member may purchase 25 or more copies for classroom use at the student discount rate (order on college letterhead).

First Printing

About the Author

Mr. Littlejohn is the deputy director of emergency management for New York City and the commanding officer of the police department's operations division. He is responsible for training, directing, and coordinating the emergency management personnel of 70 city and quasi-city agencies.

In addition, Mr. Littlejohn is a professor of organizational behavior and management at Marymount Manhattan College, New York City, and a professor of criminal justice at Jersey City State College. He is the author of numerous articles, including "Zero-Based Budgeting" and "Team Management."

Mr. Littlejohn is a Magna Cum Laude graduate of City University of New York and received his master's degree from C.W. Post College, Long Island University. He is a graduate of the Industrial College of the Armed Forces, Department of Defense University, and the U.S. Army's Command and General Staff College.

Mr. Littlejohn also serves as an independent consultant to government and industry.

Contents

1

What Is Crisis Management?

Over the past few years, government and industry have begun setting up a mechanism to identify and respond to crisis issues. For example, one of President Reagan's first acts in office was to form a crisis management team composed of the Vice President, Secretary of State, Secretary of Defense, National Security Adviser, and Director of the Central Intelligence Agency. This team was called to session for the second time in April 1982 to analyze the Falkland crisis between Argentina and Britain. The team's goal was to seek ways either to avoid the impact of this situation or mitigate its potentially destructive effects.

In addition, the industrial/business world has begun to respond to crisis issues, such as the Arab oil embargo of 1973. On June 10, 1982, the *Wall Street Journal* reported that firms are now hiring special managers for this type of troubleshooting because, according to an Atlantic Richfield executive, traditional planning staffs "didn't predict the Arab oil embargo or the environment revolution. We needed a wider, more qualitative approach to supplement the other work." (*WSJ*, June 10, 1982, p. 36, col. 3.) Basically, government and industry agree that our traditional planning staffs are, for the most part, not organized to focus on crisis issues, with some notable exceptions, such as the military.

Depending on your organizational environment, crisis issues may range from an energy emergency to the kidnapping of a CEO, from a data processing crash to an economic disaster. "Crisis" is a relative and highly subjective term that gains meaning through the individual needs of an organization and the environment in which the organization exists. Each organization formulates its own definition of a crisis by studying its own environment for potential hazards and assessing the accomplishment of organizational goals in light of them. This allows the organization to characterize as a "crisis" any event that has a direct relationship to the accomplishment of its goals.

Rather than attempt to define the many issues which could affect an organization, let's set the stage by looking briefly at a few events that have occurred—and, of course, which could occur again—in any organization.

Energy shortages. These have reverberating effects that reach into many facets of government and industry. The use of natural resources has been a substantial factor in the nation's rapid development as a world power. Starting in 1968, however, shortages in natural gas created fears that the United States' easy reliance on natural resources was at an end. As a result of the shortage, travel was restricted, causing cutbacks in many recreational activities and increasing the cost of the many needed deliveries in government and industry. Government officials, industry executives, and consumers alike became sensitive to the vulnerable position of our economy. In response, many emergency energy contingency plans were developed by various sectors of society. These plans included provisions to deal with problems in the event of an emergency. The plans also helped identify potential needs and assess the potential satisfaction of these needs.

Economic downturns. The *Wall Street Journal* on July 30, 1982, reported that "There are signs that Xerox, finally, is trying to unencumber itself. Cosmetic cost-cutting in the late 1970s failed to halt a skid in Xerox's share of the U.S. plain-paper-copier market to 42 percent last year from 67 percent in 1976, according to researchers at Dataquest Inc. Says Charles F. Christ, the head of Xerox's North American copier and duplicator manufacturing: Survival is the issue." (*WSJ*, July 30, 1982.) Many industries today are addressing the same bottom-line issue—economic survival.

Corporate theft. This practice also threatens an organization's survival. The theft of a major patent could mean economic disaster for a company. In fact, such a theft from a one-product company would virtually eliminate all thought of economic survival. In some sectors, corporate theft has become a major concern. For example, law enforcement sources have put the annual loss from corporate theft in the nation's high-tech businesses at $20 million.

Fire. On December 4, 1980, Arrow Electronics Incorporated's total sales closed at $350 million and its stock hit a high of $52.75 a share. However, the same day a flash fire exploded into an inferno at Stouffers Inn in Harrison, New York, where key executives of the major electronics company, based in Greenwich, Connecticut, were attending a budget meeting. This tragedy left 26 dead; 13 of the victims were Arrow executives.

In the days immediately following this disaster, John Waddell, Arrow's chairman, met with William Pade, a senior engagement manager at McKinsey & Co., management consultants. They began devising interim plans to run the company. They decided not to find replacements for the lost men for the first 90 days. Instead, they assembled task forces to decide the issues until the crisis situation subsided. Subsequently, according to analysts, Arrow has remained on an even keel financially, despite the widespread corporate disruption.

Natural disasters. An earthquake is one example of this type of crisis. Today, tremors and quakes occur on the West Coast with greater frequency than anywhere else in the United States. Californians breezily accept these uncontrolled disturbances as a way of life. However, elsewhere around the world, record numbers have perished: 20,000 in a 1908 earthquake that shook India; 30,000 in 1970 when quakes shook Peru; at least 1,000 persons from 1939 through 1974 in earthquakes occurring in Chile, Turkey, Ecuador, San Salvador, Nicaragua, and Pakistan; 30,000 in a 1980 earthquake in Italy; and at least 5,000 from 1962 to 1981 in Iran.

Thus, there is a broad range of situations in which both government and industry require a mechanism to identify and respond to crisis issues—a crisis management model. Some disastrous situations can be avoided through planning, but other crises are unavoidable. There is not much we can do about an earthquake, for example. Crisis management techniques can only be used to ameliorate some of the destructive effects. Accordingly, in the unfortunate event of an earthquake, we should ask ourselves and our crisis management team the following single question: How many lives can be saved? The answer to this question depends on the speed of evacuation and rescue. The predictions and analysis of these evacuation procedures are the type of management required for an effective, life-saving, postcrisis scenario.

Crisis management, therefore, is a technique both for avoiding emergencies and planning for the unavoidable ones, as well as a method for dealing with them when they occur, in order to mitigate their disastrous consequences. Before analyzing the specific techniques of crisis management, we had best begin by establishing a working definition of the term. This definition can be introduced most effectively by first determining what crisis management is not.

WHAT CRISIS MANAGEMENT IS NOT

Crisis management is not mismanagement. Often, as a result of inappropriate planning or the absence of any kind of planning at all, organizations engage in constant crisis-type situational reactions. Without ordered priorities, an organization never knows which situations call for immediate attention and which do not. As a result, they are not able to continue functioning in the face of any true crisis situation. This is mismanagement. Priorities must be ordered to enable smooth functioning in the event of an actual crisis. Crisis management should be a systematic approach for handling real crises in such a manner that the organization can continue to function normally.

Crisis management is not a quick-fix solution. It entails identifying, studying, and forecasting crisis issues, and setting forth specific ways that would enable an organization to prevent or cope with crises. This is a long-term commitment.

Crisis management is not solely represented by a separate functional organizational unit. It is a conglomerate of organizational units perceived to be necessary to manage a particular crisis. The crisis management team is the pivotal element of this structure. It should not be viewed as a task force but as a permanent component of an organization that is reinforced as a matrix by functional units identified as necessary for addressing a particular crisis. The team members are not arbitrarily selected. The selection process is carried out by the crisis team manager and the functional division heads jointly. Such a dual review should ensure that the best personnel are selected for this sensitive assignment.

Finally, crisis management does not require that all personnel stop work to address each crisis. This is the antithesis of cost effectiveness. Instead, since cost effectiveness is the bottom line in both government and industry, crises should be handled with minimal interference in the day-to-day routine. Thus, the designation of a select team of individuals both to plan for and to manage the crisis represents the pinnacle of effective crisis management.

WHAT CRISIS MANAGEMENT IS

Having reviewed what crisis management is not, let's take a look at what it is. Crisis management provides an organization with a systematic, orderly response to crisis situations. This response permits the organization to continue its day-to-day business of making a profit or providing a service while the crisis is being managed. Furthermore, it creates an early detection or warning system through a finely-tuned audit mechanism. Many crises can be prevented—or at least coped with effectively—through early detection.

In addition, the organization capitalizes on the expertise of personnel from various functional areas to plan for and manage the situation. This approach is cost effective because it is based on precluding the need for a large crisis management staff. Instead, it provides a lean staff that is augmented through the "matrix organization system" (to be described fully in Chapter 3). Moreover, effectiveness is enhanced through team development, which permits multiple crises to be coordinated through an effectively functioning team.

The term "crisis management" has been selected because it can apply to a wide variety of circumstances that might disrupt the normal course of activities in various businesses, government agencies, and nonprofit enterprises.

As previously noted, the term "crisis" will vary from organization to organization. Furthermore, some organizations will prefer to replace the word "crisis" with the word "issue." Instead of calling it "crisis management," they might refer to it as "issues management." However, the label is not the important thing. What matters is pulling together effective management principles designed to identify, prevent, and manage a crisis situation. Thus, the concept of total crisis management can be envisioned in the terms of organizational design, personnel selection, team development, environmental auditing, contingency planning, and, finally, the management of the actual crisis. These concepts lay the foundation and groundwork for our crisis management model.

Chapter 2 briefly outlines what each of these elements of crisis management entails, and the following chapters deal in greater depth with each specific aspect.

2

The Crisis Management Model

The crisis management model, as depicted in Exhibit 1, represents an all-inclusive guide to approaching crisis management. It begins with the organization of a management structure and concludes with the management of the crisis itself. Each step is briefly illustrated here.

STEP 1: DESIGN THE ORGANIZATIONAL STRUCTURE

The purpose of crisis management is to utilize a lean, cost effective structure that would represent the minimum economic burden to an organization, particularly to one that is already fighting for economic survival. The crisis management matrix design, the favored structure, is composed of a lean, permanent unit augmented by expertise from various functional divisions. It is inherently flexible and quickly adaptable to changing conditions.

The matrix structure is also the most suitable one because various crisis issues may be related solely to separate and distinct organizational elements. Thus, once a crisis issue has been identified, the crisis manager can select from various functional divisions those personnel possessing the most appropriate skills and abilities to handle the situation. Having designed the organizational structure, the crisis manager is prepared to select the team.

Exhibit 1. Crisis management model.

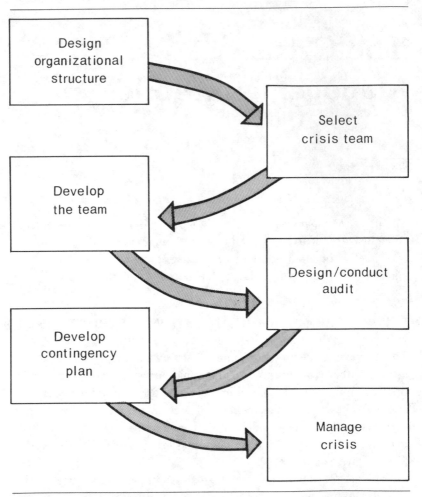

STEP 2: SELECT THE CRISIS TEAM

Crisis management team selection policies should be as similar as possible to those normally used in the organization to assign personnel to new jobs. The permanent crisis management team, in analyzing the impending crisis issue, predicts the skills needed for the project. In addition, it identifies the functional divisions from which the individuals are to be assigned and from what particular level of management they should come. In choosing which individuals to assign to the crisis team, consideration should be given to the length of the required task and to whether it will be a full- or a part-time assignment. Once the team is in place, the development process begins.

STEP 3: DEVELOP THE TEAM

After the crisis team members have been selected, the crisis team manager is responsible for developing the group into a cohesive, effective unit. In so doing, he must remember that the purpose of crisis management is to deal effectively with the crisis while allowing the remainder of the organization to perform its day-to-day routines. The process designed to transform this group of individuals (who have been selected from various functional divisions via the crisis matrix structure) into a well-organized, cohesive team is called *team development.*

Team development is accomplished by analyzing *goals* (where the team is going), *roles* (who will be doing what), and *processes* (how members will function as a team). This is undertaken by the leader, or manager, along with team members. Once team members have a complete understanding of these basics, they begin their transformation from a group of individuals into a dedicated, cohesive, functioning team. After the completion of this process, the team initiates the crisis audit.

STEP 4: DESIGN/CONDUCT A CRISIS AUDIT

The crisis audit is the foundation of the crisis management cycle. It is a tool that assists managers in systematically analyzing their environment, identifying potential issues, assessing their impact and probability of occurrence, and setting priorities among them for planning purposes. An integral part of this process is information gathering. Data should be gathered and analyzed from all possible sources.

The audit represents the data-gathering process. It is accomplished by considering both the probability of an event (threat) actually occurring and the eventual impact it would have if it did occur. For example, a utility company might have on its list of crisis issues the possibility of an accident at a nuclear facility. In conducting the audit, the team might find that although the probability of its occurrence is low, the impact of such a crisis in terms of its seriousness would be quite high. Thus, nuclear accident would probably receive a high priority on the team's crisis issue list, despite the low probability of its ever occurring.

Formulation of crisis priorities naturally follows the crisis analysis. Crisis objectives (or priorities) are not separate and distinct from organizational objectives. They run parallel to each other. Crisis objectives are designed to facilitate the accomplishment of organizational objectives by addressing the situations that would prevent the organization from reaching its goal. Furthermore, these crisis objectives are in balance with organizational objectives to the extent that they should exist only if they are used to facilitate organizational objectives at a minimum cost. Since the final objectives should reflect the thinking and inclinations of the highest levels in the organization, they should eventually be approved by the CEO or his representative. Following this approval, the crisis management team begins the contingency planning phase.

STEP 5: DEVELOP A CONTINGENCY PLAN

Once the priorities and team goals have been established, it is time to begin the crisis plan. The plan consists of five component parts: the *introduction*, the *objectives*, the *assumptions*, the *trigger mechanism*, and the *action steps*.

The *introduction* is intended to give an overview of the crisis situation. For example, a crisis plan designed to deal with a labor strike would begin with a statement identifying the union involved, the number of employees, the issues, and the date and time of the anticipated strike.

After introduction, the *objectives* of the plan should be outlined. In articulating these objectives, the manager should avoid ambiguities and generalizations, and should also state the goals as succinctly as possible.

The next component of the crisis plan involves considering the basic *assumptions*. Briefly, assumptions posit situations over which we have no control, yet which have significant impact if they occur. Assumptions should be thought of as guidelines that add both focus and depth to the objectives.

The *trigger mechanism* acts as an alarm device that activates the plan. The mechanism must be carefully constructed in order to prevent premature implementation or, conversely, delayed implementation. This mechanism can be designed to activate in a phased escalation. Although levels of activation will vary from organization to organization, the rationale behind such a system provides for enlisting only those team members and resources needed to cope with the emergency at hand. Otherwise, each incident would require a full-blown activation causing severe disruption of day-to-day operations.

Finally, upon implementation, the crisis moves to the management, or *action*, phase.

STEP 6: MANAGING THE CRISIS

At this point, it is necessary to set up some guidelines on how to actually manage the crisis.

Much, of course, will depend on the personality and style of the chief executive officer. Some CEOs might want to become directly involved, whereas others might prefer to have the crisis team manager handle the incident.

There are many ways to approach the management of crisis situations. Rather than introduce them here, they are discussed in the final chapter.

Having briefly introduced the functioning parts of the whole, let's now take a closer look at the individual phases of development in crisis management.

3

Designing the Organizational Structure

It has been recognized, over the centuries, that organizational structure facilitates the effectiveness of business. From the perspective of crisis management, the crisis structure is designed to further facilitate organizational effectiveness.

Before developing the crisis structure, we should consult with everyone in the organization who will be affected by it. Those individuals whose commitment will be needed for the future success of the crisis management team should unquestionably be consulted. Also, consideration should be given to consultation with key personnel outside the organization; that is, personnel who might have in-depth knowledge as to the strengths, weaknesses, and opportunities of the organization, and the threats to which it may be subjected. These individuals usually do not have a vested interest in any particular issue; rather, they supply objective information regarding the practicality of a proposed organizational approach.

Finally, after consulting with all personnel involved, the effects of a proposed crisis organizational structure on accomplishing overall organizational goals must be weighed. Once again, the theme of crisis management that should be stressed is maintaining the continuity of organizational goals and objectives while managing the crisis in the most expedient and cost effective method possible.

STRUCTURAL ALTERNATIVE: THE FUNCTIONAL STRUCTURE, PROS AND CONS

The functional structure is the most common and traditional form of organization. This structure organizes separate, intense groups according to function. While this structure encourages expertise and responsibility, it is very costly because it requires a myriad of specialized resources and equipment that might only be used sporadically. This over-staffing leads to inefficiency and duplication of effort. In today's economy, where government and industry must organize to reduce costs and avoid adding to the already burdensome budgets that exist, the functional structure certainly does not foster this kind of cost effectiveness.

In addition to the problem of over-staffing, the functional organization is often hampered by cumbersome communication channels. These channels often foster somewhat tenuous cooperative relations among functional divisions. This poor communication represents the antithesis of organizational team management, which requires a highly integrated information-processing system with communication lines open and functioning in all directions. Consequently, the functional structure tends to frustrate the efforts of the crisis management team.

STRUCTURAL ALTERNATIVE: THE MATRIX STRUCTURE

In the 1960s, a decade characterized by the space race and the missile gap, the aerospace industry was laced with a situation where a need for technical expertise and coordination was paramount in the organizational philosophy. As a result, the aerospace industry pioneered the matrix organizational structure. The matrix represented a new species in organizational structures.

A matrix structure is basically any organization that employs a multiple-command system—the two-boss concept. In addition to the command structure, the matrix system includes support mechanisms from functional components. These components add technical and administrative talents to the structure.

In crisis management, there is a constant need for a diversity of technical talents, expertise, and resources. The reason for this is that as the environment changes, the organizations offered must adapt their strategies to meet the changing conditions. Thus, the problem is to develop an organizational structure that will meet the ever-changing needs caused by the environment. However, such a structure must also be cost effective. Therefore, the crisis management structure should be a matrix structure that can adapt to stress and change while delivering a product with a minimum expenditure of personnel and resources.

ADVANTAGES OF A MATRIX STRUCTURE

The matrix structure gives the organization the flexibility to adapt quickly to changing conditions. It provides additional personnel where tasks are too large for the primary team members. Also, since an individual's mental capacity is finite and cannot be expert and skilled in all areas, additional expertise is often needed on a temporary basis. The matrix is able to fill this need as well.

Furthermore, an organization is constantly burdened with changing and relatively unpredictable demands. In the private sector, these demands, or crisis issues, include changes in the market, new or changing competition, technological advances, and ecological restrictions. In the public sector, they include municipal strikes, nuclear and chemical accidents, fiscal crises, and natural disasters. When these events occur, large quantities of new information must be assimilated and responded to in a coherent manner. The matrix fills this need for a highly efficient information-processing mechanism during a crisis.

In addition to the information-processing capabilities of the matrix structure, the speed and quality of decision making are also greatly enhanced. This is accomplished by using stratified channels of communication and by requiring total participation and involvement by highly qualified personnel. Within the matrix crisis organization, the selective process of obtaining the proper personnel to serve on a crisis team ensures an effective balance of authority among different component members. The efficiency of the personnel enables the fulfillment of crisis-planning goals by creating complete organization support.

MATRIX CHARACTERISTICS

In sum, the following characteristics of the crisis matrix structure clearly demonstrate its advantages over the traditional model:

- Lean, cost-effective permanent staff
- Use of functional components for support and expertise
- Flexible resource allocation
- Short and direct lines of communication, both vertically and horizontally, to facilitate decision making and to respond quickly to changing needs
- Broader vision by using functional managers who serve on the crisis team
- Support from the highest level
- Efficient and cost effective to design and implement

The advantages of the matrix become even more apparent upon analyzing the model in both a public and private setting.

THE MATRIX MODEL: THE PUBLIC SECTOR

Exhibit 2 represents a model for a municipal crisis matrix organization. As depicted, the organization is headed by a mayor, the equivalent of the private sector's chief executive officer. Various functional components (fire, police, transportation, and so on) report to the mayor, and each component is responsible only for functions within its respective area. In addition to the various functional components, the mayor has a crisis management team reporting directly to him.

The crisis management team is reinforced as a matrix in that it draws resources as needed from the other functional components. To show the dependency of the team on other functional components, let's consider a strike by private carters (sanitation workers). In both planning and managing the crisis, the crisis team would need technical and managerial assistance from the following agencies:

Exhibit 2. Public sector matrix.

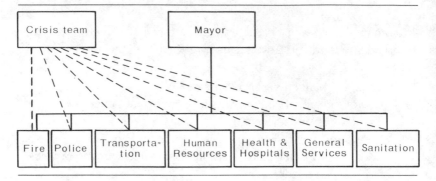

Fire: To serve summonses for violations and address hazards resulting from the strike.

Health: To issue certificates of health hazard so that municipal sanitation can be used to pick up commercial refuse.

Sanitation: To pick up refuse at commercial establishments based on the certificate of health or fire emergency.

Police: To provide protection to nonstriking municipal sanitation personnel collecting refuse that has created a fire or health hazard at commercial establishments.

Transportation: To provide traffic control during mass refuse pick-up.

The sanitation workers' strike represents a brief scenario of one type of crisis that could confront municipal government. The matrix structure seems highly appropriate for handling such a situation. Consider, however, the enormous problems in coordination and communication this crisis would present to a mayor operating with a functional organizational structure. In such a structure, each functional component head would report directly to the mayor, with each agency addressing individual needs resulting from the crisis. The mayor would wind up with five individual plans rather than one plan outlining a comprehensive course of action.

Under the crisis matrix structure, however, the crisis team manager would coordinate the development of one comprehensive plan and direct the management of the crisis. This facilitates communication up, down, and across the organization. This, of course, also permits the mayor to address the more global issues of the crisis and prevents him from becoming bogged down with noncritical details.

THE MATRIX MODEL: THE PRIVATE SECTOR

Exhibit 3 represents a private sector matrix model. It parallels the public model in that the crisis team is supplemented with resources from the functional divisions. It should be noted that this model can be used for any type of crisis, ranging from natural gas decontrol to a major strike that could cripple a corporation.

Using the labor issue as an example, let's examine the workings of such a matrix structure. The crisis team would conduct an assessment to determine the probability of a strike and design a contingency plan to cope with it. Personnel from the various functional units would be temporarily assigned to the crisis team for technical assistance and support. Some of their functions would include the following tasks:

Exhibit 3. Private sector matrix.

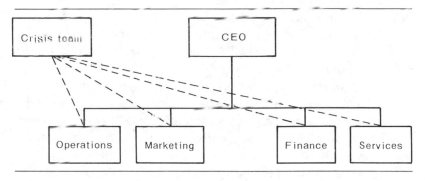

Operations: To decipher priority services and plan for their maintenance by management and other nonstriking personnel.

Marketing: To assess the impact of a strike on the consumer and relate its findings to operations, which can then set priorities as to which services to maintain.

Finances: To assess the short- and long-term financial impact of the strike on the organization.

It should be apparent that the matrix structure is equally appropriate for both the public and private sectors. The bi-level analysis of a crisis situation enables more precise and comprehensive decision making under either model. For the most part, the difference between the two sectors is in their goals—service versus profits. But regardless of the goal, the basic crisis management principles are the same.

THE CRISIS MANAGEMENT TEAM: AN EXAMPLE

The crisis management team can take many configurations. One option is to subdivide the team into three parts: the policy team, the management team, and the liaison team. Not all crises will necessitate activating all three teams. Most minor crises can be managed quite adequately by the management team alone.

The policy team, which has a chairperson and a director, is composed of the top-level executives. Its function is to set broad policy guidelines that direct the management team in handling the crisis. Policy issues must be identified and clarified early in the planning phase. This will ensure that the plans developed and implemented are in accord with the desires of the CEO. The policy team is ordinarily an ad hoc group chaired by the CEO.

The management team consists of planners and managers who are assigned on either a full- or part-time basis. However, at least some members of the team should be assigned full-time. The management team's function is to identify issues with crisis potential and design plans to mitigate, manage, and recover from any crisis. It must be stressed that these personnel are not only *planning* for the crisis but will also be responsible for *managing* it if it occurs. This ensures a total commitment to the organization. In addition to the functions just cited, the management team is responsible for directing, coordinating, and managing the liaison team.

The liaison team is composed of personnel representing either divisions or departments within a particular organization, or personnel from other agencies or organizations. Their assignment to the crisis team is facilitated by the matrix structure. For example, in a municipal agency, the liaison team would be composed of representatives from various agencies; that is, transportation, fire, police, sanitation, highways, hospitals, and so on. On the other hand, in the private sector, the liaison team might consist of representatives from marketing, finance, production, legal, management information systems, personnel, and so on. These team members take on dual functions: first, they lend expertise to the crisis management team while planning for or managing an actual crisis; second, they are responsible for keeping their respective departments or divisions informed regarding the crisis management program.

This three-pronged crisis management model has proved very effective in New York City. Within the city there is a Mayor's Emergency Control Board, which represents the crisis policy team. It is composed of the mayor, as chairman; the police commissioner, as director; and various commissioners and heads of both public and private organizations. Its function is to formulate policy to deal with emergencies. The second prong is the crisis management team. It is represented by the Office of Civil Preparedness, which is composed of planners and managers who work full-time at planning and managing crises. Lastly, the liaison team is composed of liaison personnel from the various city agencies as dictated by the crisis at hand.

It should be emphasized that each of the three respective teams—policy, management, and liaison—has a crucial role in the total crisis management process. Furthermore, like vital organs of the human body, one team cannot function effectively without the others.

4

Selecting a Crisis Team

Having designed the organizational structure, we can turn to the next order of business: selecting a crisis team. But first, the CEO must appoint a crisis team manager. The success or failure of the entire crisis management operations rests on the selection.

THE CRISIS MANAGER

At a minimum, the crisis team manager should possess the following characteristics. He or she must:

- Be able to adopt and support the team management philosophy
- Be a strong "team player"
- Have the ability to delegate
- Be a strong communicator
- Have a high degree of salesmanship talent
- Be a strong decision-maker
- Possess excellent judgment
- Be an expert at time management.

Each of these characteristics warrants separate discussion.

First and foremost, the individual selected as the crisis team manager must be one who has adopted or is willing to adopt the philosophy of team management. This is crucial because the crisis management environment is a unique situation. Identifying crisis issues, preparing contingency plans, and managing a crisis require dealing with personnel drawn from a multitude of different organizational components. These individuals cannot function effectively as a group unless they are formed into a smooth-running, cohesive team. The crisis manager, as the leader of that team, must be a supporter of the team philosophy.

A second trait necessary for a competent team manager is that he or she be a team player. The importance of this has been exemplified in a recent situation within the Reagan administration. As mentioned at the outset of this briefing, President Reagan has a crisis management team because the Reagan administration places a high priority on teamwork. Alexander Haig, former secretary of state, was a member of this crisis management team. However, according to many political observers, Haig was not a team player. As a result, his interaction with the team was not harmonious and in some cases was actually considered counterproductive. Thus, the Reagan crisis management team was not functioning as effectively as it could have been. The importance of this managerial characteristic is further emphasized by the fact that the person chosen to replace Haig has a reputation as a team player.

A good team leader also must have the ability to delegate. Delegation is basic to effective team management. The crisis matrix model provides the crisis team with the tool to reassign resources from the various functional components. It is primarily up to the crisis team manager to delegate to individuals tasks that are within their particular specialty. A strong crisis team manager will delegate, coordinate, and control.

When delegation is well planned and carefully thought out, the personnel selectively assigned feel more comfortable in their roles. This allows a feeling of trust to develop. Trust, in turn, opens up avenues of communication, both vertically and horizontally, throughout the organization. This brings us to our next important characteristic of a crisis manager: He or she must be a good communicator.

Often, in management consultation, you will find that problems which are initially diagnosed as major organizational obstructions requiring severe adjustments turn out to be simply problems of poor communication.

Moreover, once a crisis situation actually occurs, poor communication will compound existing problems. The crisis manager must convey clear, concise, and specific information to all concerned. Often, those people with whom the crisis manager communicates are people he or she does not have authority over; thus, the manager must possess a high degree of salesmanship ability.

Salesmanship talent is essential. It enables the manager to be effective in areas where he or she possesses no authority. The crisis manager's ability to influence personnel from other functional divisions within the organization and key personnel outside the organization plays an important role in overall effectiveness. In private sector organizations, he or she may have to deal with personnel from municipal, state, and federal agencies, whereas in public section organizations, the crisis manager may work with personnel from various private sector organizations. Without salesmanship expertise, the manager may easily alienate one or more of these agencies by overstepping his or her authority. This, of course, could seriously impede the crisis management process.

In the crisis environment, there is no place for procrastination. The crisis manager must have the ability to make good decisions, quickly. Since the potential for harm is always present in a crisis situation, a *good* decision executed immediately is better than a *perfect* decision executed too late. Indecision on the part of a crisis manager is cause for immediate replacement. The strong decision-maker must take calculated risks while exercising good judgment.

This brings us to yet another characteristic of a good crisis manager: He or she must have excellent judgment. "Judgment," as defined in *Webster's New Collegiate Dictionary,* is the "mental capacity of deciding correctly by the comparison of facts and ideas." This is a quality that is difficult to evaluate during an interview. However, it is one that is readily apparent when observing managers at work. It may take a little longer to find a manager who possesses good judgment, but it's well worth the trouble. Judgment is an indispensable quality in a crisis situation and one that should be highly regarded in the selection of a crisis manager.

Finally, the crisis manager must practice the principles of good time management. The manager will be inundated with an enormous volume of information, requests, and projects for development. He or she must list tasks and follow up on them. Under the plan presented here, the manager creates a list of things to be completed every day, in order of highest to lowest priority. The item of first priority is attacked immediately. Once that item is completed, then number two and then three receive attention. This procedure is performed each day. It requires constant direction and provides for immediate results.

Exhibit 4 further describes the duties and responsibilities of a crisis manager.

In selecting a crisis manager, it is worth remembering that he or she must report directly to the CEO. This direct contact is necessary due to

Exhibit 4. Crisis manager: Position description*

Position: Crisis manager
Reports to: CEO

Primary objective

Directs and coordinates the organization's crisis management program. Conducts crisis audits, defines crisis goals and objectives, and provides leadership in the preparation of plans for their achievement.

Responsibilities

1. Assists the president and members of the executive team in analyzing organizational objectives and goals in light of crisis issues.
2. Designs the crisis management organization, selects and trains personnel.
3. Designs and coordinates a crisis management audit program.
4. Develops and establishes priorities among organizational crisis objectives and directs the preparation of contingency plans.
5. Undertakes special studies requested by the CEO.
6. Monitors, investigates, and assesses external threats to the organization.
7. Assists other departments and divisions of the organization in assessing crisis issues in their planning activities.
8. Maintains contacts with industry, government, and the academic community for the purpose of fostering exchange of information.
9. Establishes productive work relations between crisis management team and major organizational components.
10. Collaborates with fellow executives in the selection of liaison personnel to serve on the crisis management team.

*SOURCE: Eagle Associates Inc.

the sensitivity of the work that the crisis manager performs, and because the issues are often organization-wide in scope. Ideally, the crisis manager should be on a level equivalent to a vice president. This puts the manager on equal footing with other functional organizational heads. As a high-ranking individual reporting directly to the CEO, the crisis manager will be able to address and resolve the critical issues affecting the organization without encumbrances.

Depending on the crisis project, the crisis team manager must perform a job analysis to determine the tasks, duties, and responsibilities to be carried out. This entails a systematic investigation to determine the requirements and qualifications of the personnel needed to perform the crisis function. Job analysis leads to the development of job descriptions and job specifications. The by-product of it all will be job evaluations.

The job description represents a summary of the tasks, duties, and responsibilities of the position. Also, it includes what has to be done, why, and how long it is expected to take. The job description also includes the performance standards, which are the parameters of satisfactory performance in each area.

The job specifications include the various qualifications, skills, and experience needed to perform the responsibilities outlined. These specifications will be used in selecting and recruiting the people to fill the various spots.

MANAGEMENT TEAM

It is the responsibility of the crisis manager to select the permanent cadre of personnel who will make up the management team. Some of the personal characteristics we look for in selecting a crisis manager also apply to the management team personnel; for example, team player, good communicator, good judgment, and good manager of time. In addition, the team members should be selected from a cross-section of the organization. Since the management team must initially identify crisis issues that affect the organization as a whole, broadly based organizational knowledge is desirable.

Finally, members of the management team must have good planning skills. Conducting crisis audits and developing contingency plans represent major responsibilities.

As the management team identifies crisis issues via its audit function, the crisis manager begins formulating the crisis project. An important part of this task is selecting members of the liaison team. As previously indicated, the liaison team consists of personnel from various functional divisions throughout the organization.

LIAISON TEAM

The liaison team is an integral component of the crisis management process. These personnel bring expertise, values, and priorities from various parts of the organization. In addition, they serve as a vital communication link with their division or unit.

Our crisis matrix provides for the temporary or permanent assignment of liaison personnel from different divisions to the crisis management team. This procedure facilitates and strengthens communication within the organization.

The individual selection and assignment process should be a joint decision of the crisis manager and the functional division head to which the team member belongs. Furthermore, the manager and division head should mutually agree on the duration and other details of the assignments.

5

Developing the Team

Although the matrix organization has many advantages, it will always be a high-tension system—one that places great demands on people. In this context, teamwork is crucial. Once the members of the team have been selected, the crisis manager, as team developer, must spend the time necessary to transform this collection of individuals into a cohesive and effective unit.

This chapter defines one concept of team management, outlines the benefits of this type of set-up, and describes the characteristics of an effective organizational team. The discussion also offers a model for building a crisis management team. It may make things clearer if we begin by clearing away some misconceptions about team building.

WHAT TEAM DEVELOPMENT IS NOT

Team development is not a short-term task. It is a long-range philosophy of management that permeates an organization and actually becomes a collective state of mind. Techniques such as goal setting, decision making, conflict resolution, and communication must be constantly worked on and perfected. The team members must apply critical judgment to their actions and must seek to improve themselves on a daily basis. Only in this way will the team be prepared to function smoothly and effectively in a crisis.

Team development is not a canned seminar. It is a workshop that the crisis manager should tailor to the needs of the organization. Organizational problems are diagnosed by means of group discussion and ongoing group feedback. Once the problems are specified, the group should begin working to improve inadequate skills or operations. Those skills that need work can range from goals and roles and relationships to intergroup friction.

Team development is not a staff responsibility. It is the line manager's responsibility; in our case, it is the crisis manager's responsibility. The crisis manager must be astute in identifying and solving problems. Furthermore, he or she must be a team leader who will take responsibility for conducting weekly or bi-weekly team meetings. At these meetings the team members discuss where they stand on their goals, how the team performs such functions as making decisions and resolving conflict, and the status of individual staff responsibility. This, again, is a long-term responsibility for a line manager.

Team development is not a panacea for all organizational ills. Problems will not disappear just by implementing the concept. It will, however, refine an organization's diagnostic skills and increase its ability to devise solutions.

Team development is not an abrogation of managerial responsibility. While the team management philosophy calls for a high degree of delegation, it is not meant to be a managerial tool to avoid decision-making. The primary purpose of team management is to encourage dedication on the part of all team members.

Most of all, team development is not easy. It is a long-term commitment that requires a lot of work. However, the eventual benefits far outweigh the effort invested.

WHAT TEAM DEVELOPMENT IS

Team development is a ongoing process of transforming a group of individuals into an effectively functioning team. This is accomplished through the fine-tuning of feedback, problem solving, goal setting, and evaluation.

Feedback is essential in team management, although it is often neglected. It involves constant communication among team members.

Questions such as "What am I doing wrong in this situation?" frequently come up. Team members should constructively criticize each other to pinpoint problem areas. On the basis of such criticism, the team begins to identify and diagnose problems—potential or actual—in its own operations.

Through the use of such feedback, the team can set improvement goals for solving identified problems. For example, the team members might ask themselves, "How can we do this better next time?" Once that question is answered, the team attempts to perfect its performance, and the process begins all over again. This creates an environment that is constantly improving. The status quo is never merely accepted, and performances are evaluated and re-evaluated on an ongoing basis.

BENEFITS OF TEAM MANAGEMENT

Team development improves communication. Communication is the most important element of a successful organization. Without it, roles are not clarified, goals are not set properly, and conflict is not resolved. When people begin communicating as a team, understanding improves. Deeper understanding, in turn, breaks down the barriers to communication. Thus, interaction is enhanced. As a result, the team members become more open with each other, and a feeling of trust evolves. Trust is an essential prerequisite to communication. Distrust is, in the end, destructive to organizational affairs.

One area of communication that is highly important is the art of listening. A study done at the University of Michigan on communication revealed that we write approximately 9 percent of the time, read about 16 percent of the time, talk to each other about 30 percent of the time, and listen 45 percent of the time. It is essential that when we are listening, we actual "hear" and understand what the other person is saying. This skill should be cultivated to increase the team's effectiveness.

Team development makes it possible to resolve conflicts openly and constructively through the use of expanded communication systems. By improving communication, team members can better understand what their conflicts are and go about resolving them more effectively. Within the team concept, members confront conflict immediately and handle it directly. Other systems sweep over conflict and pretend it doesn't exist until it is too late.

Team development creates better problem-solvers. First of all, the number of potential solutions increases proportionately with the number of people working on them. Secondly, along with this multitude of ideas, people working as a team usually become greater risk-takers. When people know that they do not have to make a decision alone, they will very often throw out ideas of greater creativity than if functioning independently. Finally, as a result of this participative atmosphere, team members feel a greater sense of involvement and, as a result, greater commitment to the organization.

Team development improves cooperation and coordination among employees. This is a by-product of improved communications and open resolution of conflicts. Team members feel a loyalty to the team, which increases their interest in cooperating with fellow co-workers. As a result of the group's willingness to cooperate with each other, intergroup activities are much better coordinated.

Team development increases employee job satisfaction. Individual employees are no longer just individuals. They are now members of an effectively functioning team. Whenever a decision is reached or a goal achieved, they can feel as though they had something to do with it. Team members gain individual satisfaction from each team accomplishment. Each team member lends information and expertise to the group and is, therefore, appreciated for his or her value to the entire organization.

Team development induces ambitious goal striving. Since team members have greater risk taking abilities than do individuals working alone, they will, similarly, assume more ambitious goals. Team members become motivated to pursue success rather than avoid failure. Individual employees feel secure with a team behind them and gain a sense of confidence that enables them to set and achieve more ambitious goals.

Finally, the most important feature of team development is that it increases productivity. As members of the team fine tune their various skills, they begin to identify with the organization's goals. This creates a commitment to working toward these shared goals—the one working ingredient necessary for increased productivity.

CHARACTERISTICS OF AN EFFECTIVE TEAM

To summarize, there are five necessary characteristics of an effective team:

1. The team should have a high level of communication. This is listed first because it is probably one of the most important and most neglected aspects of American organizations today. Communication should be both vertical and horizontal; that is, team members should feel free to discuss all matters with their superiors and subordinates as well as with their colleagues. Also, team members should engage in intergroup communication.

2. An effective team is characterized by a high level of trust among employees. This trust develops from in-depth communication among team members that eventually permeates the organization. Since our crisis matrix provides for a liaison team made up of personnel from different divisions, it is relatively easy to strengthen communication throughout the organization.

3. Involvement is also a key team characteristic. Team members should be involved in goal setting, role clarification, problem diagnosis, conflict resolution, and decision making.

4. As previously noted, involvement creates a sense of commitment to the organization. Therefore, commitment is also an important team characteristic. This commitment is exemplified by the fact that *I*'s and *my*'s are replaced with *we*'s and *our*'s. Team members forgo egotism and start thinking in terms of the group.

5. The last team characteristic is a high degree of delegation. We cannot have a successful team when the team manager attempts to handle everything. The managers should not sign every routine document, nor should he or she be involved in every minute decision. The authority to conduct these affairs should be delegated to various team members. This is something to which team managers must become accustomed.

We have defined what team development is, what it is not, and the benefits and characteristics of an effective team. Now, let's review the area of team dynamics.

TEAM DYNAMICS

Team dynamics consists of those variables that represent the necessary ingredients for effective team development. The crisis manager must continually observe and fine tune team dynamics, which are represented by its *goals, roles, processes,* and *relationships.*

Goals. These must be specific, understandable, and clearly communicated to all team members. Communication is important because team goals must be shared by all. For example, an organization's finance people might eliminate two financial analysts in order to cut costs. At the same time, however, the crisis manager might take on a very ambitious goal requiring more financial analysts. Since this could cause a major conflict in the organization, goals must be developed and communicated.

Roles. Role conflict and role ambiguity are two of the most serious sources of organizational stress. It is important, therefore, to identify and refine roles and clear up any possible causes for confusion.

Processes. This covers how the team functions; for example, how decisions are made, what leadership style prevails, and how the team conducts its meetings.

Consider for a moment team decision making. In a highly effective team, individual members feel secure about making decisions, and the decisions seem appropriate to them because they clearly understand the goals and philosophy of operations. Such understanding provides a solid base for decisions. This unleashes initiative while still maintaining a coordinated and directed effort.

The decision-making process used by many teams to make full use of available resources is consensus. With consensus, each team member should be able to accept the team decision on the basis of logic and feasibility. The crisis manager's leadership style is paramount in this whole process.

The leadership role in team building is a delicate one, because it should not be heavy-handed and should be shared with team members. The formal leader reflects and clarifies organizational policy, but at times other team members may take the lead in sharpening points or in supplying information. Actually, in the team context, one person is rarely capable of meeting all the leadership needs of a particular team.

The leader's role involves strengthening the team and the team's processes by ensuring that members deal with all problems that confront them.

Relationships. Since we all have different values, personalities, and styles, it is important to analyze and work on the way we relate to each other. Good communication will improve relationships, as will honesty and trust among team members.

One aspect of team relationships that deserves special attention is conflict. In most organizations, conflict among team members is a frequent occurrence. Members can differ in their interests, perceptions, and (quite possibly) in their ideas on how certain issues should be handled. And this conflict can range from mild disagreement to outright wrangling and hostility. If the crisis team is to function smoothly, it is imperative that team members find a way to deal with conflict.

Denial, avoidance, suppression, and compromise are all means of dealing with conflict. Alternatively, the conflict can be accepted and worked through. Avoiding conflict at all costs may sound like a good solution, but it can actually have a destructive effect on team building, because it tends to deprive team members of needed information. (The Bay of Pigs disaster during the Kennedy administration is often cited as an example of the consequence of too little conflict. The National Security Council suppressed critical information rather than confront disagreement.) On the other hand, struggling with conflict fosters involvement, exchange of information, and ultimately better decisions for the team.

Conflict can be either good or bad. The leader must continually monitor and evaluate how his or her teammates are handling it.

THE WORKSHOP

The initial step in fostering team dynamics is to conduct a team-building workshop. In doing so, there are several important points to keep in mind.

Setting. The workshop setting is an integral part of the team-building process. The workshop must not be perceived as "business as usual."

Instead, the setting should be comfortable, informal, and interruption-free. In fact, it may be best to leave the business location altogether. Meetings conducted away from the business environment are generally taken more seriously by personnel. They also are more relaxed and conducive to the free exchange of ideas.

If it is not possible to leave the office, then the best alternative is a conference room without telephones. No interruptions should be permitted.

Composition. The team must be assembled with great care. It should have no more than 12 to 15 members; larger groups have a tendency to break up into competing subgroups. On the other hand, too few members may result in a loss of the "synergism" that is so vital to a team's success. Of course, team size will depend, to a degree, on the particular mission. But some guidelines are important, inasmuch as team effectiveness will be strongly influenced by team size.

Structure. The workshop should be divided into two one-day sessions. The first day is designed to discuss perceptions of the organization and the team members themselves. Members exchange opinions, thoughts, ideas, and feelings about the organization as a place to work. Team members need an opportunity to gain information about one another—an area often overlooked in day-to-day work.

The second day focuses on planning and goal setting. The areas that shoud be addressed are: mission (why do we exist?); situation (where are we now?); and strategies (how are we going to reach our goals?). The answers to these questions help provide the basis for contingency plans, as well as for common understanding and commitment from an involved team.

The crisis team leader must have some type of script or model from which to work in orchestrating the workshop.

THE TEAM DEVELOPMENT MODEL

The first step is a basic *introduction* that acts as an "ice breaker." Team members are given an overview of the team process. In order to become comfortable with their co-workers, team members should discuss a few things about themselves that could be important to the whole group. This creates a relaxed atmosphere and gives team members a chance to understand more about one another.

The next step is to set up ground rules. These rules establish the overall functioning procedures that will be followed. Meeting attendance, co-worker respect, and manner of decision making are among the items that might be discussed.

Data gathering comes next. This is essentially to pinpointing the problems the team has to tackle. These problems could range from an unclear goal to a conflict in roles to a severe personality clash.

After information on organizational problems has been gathered, it is the team's obligation to *identify, analyze* and then *diagnose* these problems. By first identifying a problem and then analyzing it, the team can usually formulate an appropriate diagnosis. Information about this diagnosis is fed from individual team members to the entire group so that the group can formulate an action plan to cope with the problem.

The team can be divided into individual groups to work on certain problems. The proposals are then presented to the entire team, which collectively creates an *action plan*. This action plan should indicate what the options are, what is going to be done, and who is going to do it.

Finally, the team should *evaluate its effectiveness*. This is accomplished through the use of team meetings to discuss the results of the action plan. Such a team evaluation focuses on whether or not there has been organizational improvement. The answer to that question is important because it aids the team in making future plans. If a plan has been ineffective, the team will not use it again. If it has been successful, then it will be used as a model for future plans.

In addition to the day-to-day attention given to the team process, some teams schedule weekly team meetings for follow-ups. It is a good idea to rotate the chairperson for each team meeting so that a different member takes responsibility for the agenda and the discussion during each week's meeting. It is important to schedule at least ten minutes to evaluate the process. This evaluation uncovers problem areas, suggests solutions, and strengthens the team bond.

6

The Crisis Audit

Thus far we have designed our organization and selected our personnel. Now we are ready to study the three operational aspects of crisis management: the crisis audit, the crisis contingency plan, and the actual crisis management. Let's begin by looking at the crisis audit.

Contingency plans can be made only after undertaking a thorough analysis of the crisis issues facing the organization. Thus, the crisis audit represents a systematic approach to identifying crisis issues by gathering information on the internal and external environments and establishing priorities on these issues. This is done by analyzing their probability and possible impact.

To facilitate this task, the crisis audit is divided into two parts. Part one is designed to identify the crisis issues via information gathering Part two will assess these issues according to their impact on the organization and their probability of occurrence.

In identifying crisis issues, the organization must gather information related to its strengths, weaknesses, and threats. Strengths are those qualities that make the organization profitable or facilitate delivery of a high-quality service. A strength of IBM, for example, might be its technical expertise, which, in conjunction with its marketing, delivers service to a huge clientele in the data processing industry. Similarly, in the health-care industry, a strength might be a modernized ambulance fleet equipped with emergency medical technicians capable of delivering a high-quality service to many individuals.

Although each organization has strengths, it also has inherent weaknesses that detract from its mission and, in some cases, even precipitate disaster. Weaknesses, of course, are those organizational or environmental characteristics that inhibit or limit the achievement of organizational goals. For example, a computer firm operating without a back-up system and/or duplicate data in storage could, during a power outage, lose vital information. This would represent a distinct weakness that could bring virtual disaster to the company. Similarly, a fire department operating in a large metropolitan area with high-rise buildings would have a distinct weakness if it lacked a helicopter service to transport firefighters to the rooftops during a fire. This particular weakness, of course, is one of those that could easily lead to disaster on a grand scale.

Threats represent internal or external events that could seriously affect an organization's ability to produce profit or deliver services. An organization that produces only one product would consider the theft of its patent as an extremely serious threat. Such an act of industrial sabotage could virtually put an organization out of business. For a municipal government, a severe snow storm or blizzard represents a threat necessitating contingency plans. To assist the crisis team in its information-gathering process, let's look at a few methods in use.

INFORMATION GATHERING

There are two methods by which we can gather information, both internally and externally. One is through existing published data, including newspapers, periodicals, government documents, and university publications. Government agencies provide statistics relating to almost every area of business. For example, *The Mini-Guide to the Economic Census*, published by the U.S. Department of Commerce/Social and Economic Statistics Administration/Bureau of the Census, lists sources available to help gather statistics on retail trade, wholesale trade, construction industries, mineral industries, transportation, manufacturing, and other related economic information.

Second, the organization can compile its own statistics, through discussions with key people and groups within the company, reference to corporate-planning documents, meetings with trade association representatives, and discussions with professional consultants and with corporate counterparts in other companies. Probably, the group holding the key to many issues is your own personnel. Often overlooked in the consulting process, these individuals possess a wealth of knowledge and experience.

Having gathered data on organizational strengths, weaknesses, and threats, we are ready to enter part two of our crisis audit: What will the impact be if a threat does arise and what is the probability of its actually occurring?

DETERMINING IMPACT

In determining the impact of a potential crisis, we must analyze the various threats. We must consider the possibility of a particular threat developing into a crisis. More specifically, we must consider what will happen to the people and property in a given area if this threat does materialize.

There are various factors to consider in determining impact. Among them are the extent of physical injury (be it personal or property damage), costs to the organization and society, time needed for recovery, prospective future complications resulting from the event, and the psychological ramifications within society as a whole. The last factor includes the element of public reaction. An event may not cause a great deal of physical damage, but it may create public fear. This definitely increases the impact of the event.

Let's take this last point one step further. The threat of a crisis—whether the dangers are real or imagined—can cause public fear, and this, in turn, can have a serious impact on an organization. In the private sector, for example, marketing people have seen good products destroyed because of public fear of imagined consequences. Similarly, in the public sector organizations have had their reputations tarnished and programs destroyed because of public fear.

Having carefully reviewed the impact of each crisis issue, we are ready to determine the probability of a crisis occurring.

DETERMINING PROBABILITY

Probability is measured as the number of ways a particular event can result from certain activity, divided by the total number of results possible from the occurrence of that activity. More specifically, with regard to crisis assessment, probability is defined as the number of times per given time period that a crisis event will occur. A general formula for calculating such a rating would be: $P = X/N$, where X is the number of outcomes favoring a possible event and N equals the total number of outcomes. P, of course, is the probability of an event occurring.

For example, in assessing the probability of a hazardous materials spill, N would be the total number of times a particular organization transports hazardous materials in one year. X would be the number of spills or accidents that occurred in that year. If materials were transported 100 times in a year and there was only one spill, the probability of a spill could be assessed at one percent.

$$X = 1$$
$$N = 100$$
$$P = 1/100 = 1.00\%$$

However, even with such a formula available, we must often resort to other forms of calculations. This occurs in assessing events that are unprecedented or rare (such as a nuclear accident). Without historical data to plug into the formula, it is virtually useless. On the other hand, relatively frequent crisis events (such as airplane crashes, hazardous material spills, and economic fluctuations) facilitate use of such a probability formula.

In the case of a rare event, we must resort to another type of analysis. We must analyze conditions surrounding the possible occurrence of this rare crisis and determine the different ways it can occur. To do this, the analysis is shifted to the circumstances surrounding the occurrence of the event. By determining the probability of these conditions, we have a more concrete standard with which to assess the potential hazard. Certain social and political disruptions, for example, might increase the probability of the event occurring.

It must be emphasized that this type of assessment involves the element of judgment to a greater extent than does the strictly mathematical calculation. It must also be emphasized that the primary purpose of assessing both impact and probability is so that priorities can be set and countermeasures devised.

ESTABLISHING PRIORITIES

Thus, by weighing the two factors—impact and probability—we reach an assessment for a particular crisis event. If the assessment for an event is high, then there is a more urgent need to plan for its occurrence. Conversely, if it is low, there is less need to plan for it. To enable quick reference to the different vulnerability levels, it is essential to list these potential crisis events in order of severity. The ranking descends in order from the most serious risk to the least serious risk. The event should be listed with reference to both its impact and its probability.

With this accomplished, crisis planners have their work laid out for them. They begin developing contingency plans for the event having the highest vulnerability assessment and work their way down the list.

7

The Crisis Contingency Plan

Organizations today, whose success or failure depends on the ability to achieve their organizational goals, must plan for crisis contingencies. Few organizations viewed the 1974 recession as a crisis until it was too late. However, several organizations, through crisis contingency planning, were better prepared to withstand the problems associated with the 1979–80 recession.

The basic purpose of crisis planning is to increase managerial effectiveness in achieving organizational goals. Crisis planning serves to optimize performance in a changing environment. As we saw in the last chapter in our discussion of the management audit, this process forces an organization to take a hard look at its internal and external environments.

Contingency planning begins with the premise that a crisis issue may hinder successful achievement of an organizational goal. Thus, a contingency plan is simply the process of considering hypothetical situations and alternative scenarios that might occur in a specific organizational setting. Before getting into the development of such a plan, however, let's take a look at some of the characteristics that make up an effective contingency plan:

- The plan must be doable. If a plan cannot be effectively implemented and carried out, it is not worth the paper it is written on,
  no matter how elaborate it is.
- The plan must be understandable. It should be written to accom-
  modate all levels of intelligence in an organization. Keep it simple.
- The plan must be comprehensive. A good plan should contain
  enough material to make sure it is carried out effectively. Too
  much detail becomes burdensome and represents an impediment
  to implementation.
- The plan must be approved. This approval should encompass all
  personnel who are affected by the plan.
- The plan must be reviewed. The review must be performed reg-
  ularly to prevent obsolescence.
- The plan must be tested. This will ensure that all players understand their respective roles.
- The plan must be cost effective. The cost incurred by the planning
  project must outweigh the consequences of not planning.

Now, let's review the components of our crisis plan—introduction,
objectives, assumptions, trigger mechanisms, and operating structure.

THE CRISIS PLAN

The introduction is intended to provide an overview of the situation.
For example, a crisis plan designed to deal with an inflammatory labor
situation would begin with a statement identifying the union involved,
the number of employees, the issues, and the date and time of the
anticipated strike.

A specific and succinct outline of the objectives of the plan follows
the introduction. The objectives should be concrete and workable and
should avoid ambiguities and generalizations. Continuing with the labor
scenario, the first objective of the plan might be to maintain the continuity of service at a 25 percent reduction. This objective is specific,
concrete, concise, and it is hoped, doable.

Assumptions represent the next component of the crisis plan. Assumptions posit hypothetical situations over which we have no control,

yet which will have significant impact if they occur. For example, one assumption might be that a strike will last 90 days. We might base this assumption upon past experience with the union involved or with unions of a similar trade. Another assumption might be that acts of sabotage will take place. Once again, these are things over which we have no control, but which have a serious impact on business. Assumptions can be thought of as guidelines that give both focus and depth to our objectives.

In designating assumptions, the crisis planner should remember three rules:

- Assumptions must be realistic.
- Assumptions must be stated positively, using the word "will."
- Assumptions should be made only after thorough research.

After carefully delineating the assumptions of a crisis plan, the planner can now design the *trigger mechanism*.

The trigger mechanism can be thought of as an alarm device that activates the plan. This mechanism must be carefully constructed to prevent premature implementation or implementation after the fact. Premature implementation could actually bring about an event that otherwise might not occur. For example, triggering a labor contingency plan prematurely, during sensitive negotiations, could cause an all-out strike. On the other hand, delayed implementation could preclude effective handling of the labor issue.

The trigger mechanism can also be designed in a phased escalation. Each phase escalates with the intensity of the incident. For example, some contingency plans are designed with a three-phase trigger mechanism: Phase I, the monitoring phase, is normally triggered in anticipation of an incident; Phase II, the activation of the plan, calls for the mobilization of the management and liaison teams; Phase III, the most serious, activates the policy team.

The information-gathering process carried out during the audit provides the data needed to design the trigger mechanism. For example, if an organization identifies an economic crisis issue, a host of economic indicators would be monitored to provide the necessary data for analysis.

Finally, the *operating structure*, or *action plan*, represents a series of events designed to accomplish the objectives. These steps clearly delineate the responsibilities that need to be assigned to accomplish each objective. The roles of each person, division, department, or agency must be clearly outlined. In addition, each primary role player must have a back-up or supportive role player. For example, in the public sector, the police department might play the primary role in rescuing entrapped persons, and the fire department might have the supportive role. In the private sector, the management information systems division might have overall responsibility for a communications network during an emergency and be backed up in a supportive role by the marketing division.

TESTING

Simulation testing, a recommended technique in contingency planning, is a type of dress rehearsal in which each of the players, under noncrisis conditions, walks through his or her respective role, reacting to a simulated scenario. This exercise ensures that all players are familiar with their roles and responsibilities. In addition, simulation testing uncovers areas of weakness in the contingency plan that need to be improved.

The initial simulation should be kept comparatively simple and announced in advance, giving players an opportunity to study plans. At a later date, however, an unannounced simulation exercise is recommended. This will give top management an opportunity to view the players carrying out their respective roles in a simulated scenario without prior preparation.

REVIEW

Contingency plans must be reviewed and updated. The review responsibility should be assigned to one individual, with a back-up reviewer designated to take over in case of unforeseen leave or reassignment. The organization should establish a specific time for plan review, either semiannually or annually.

A review should focus on the following questions:

1. Do the objectives still support organizational goals?
2. Are the assumptions still valid?
3. Is the triggering mechanism still appropriate?
4. Is the operating structure still workable?
5. Does the risk probability still exist?
6. Is the plan practical from a functional managerial perspective?
7. Is the plan cost effective from top management's perspective?
8. Are all personnel who have roles in implementating the plan still in their respective positions?
9. Has the plan been distributed to all personnel who need to know about it?
10. Have political priorities changed?

This review phase will not only ensure that plans remain viable and current, but also that the need for them still exists.

8

Managing the Crisis

The crisis structure has been designed, the personnel selected, the team developed, the audit conducted, and the plan developed. We have now reached the critical juncture of our crisis management program—managing the crisis.

I have found that at the outset the CEO must develop some guidelines with regard to how the actual crisis will be managed. These guidelines represent the *crisis policy*.

The policy team assists the CEO in policy formulation. The team consists of key executives whose interactions are essential in managing a particular crisis. It is important to keep this team limited to the absolutely essential people, thus preventing the group from subdividing into smaller groups. Such factionalism would only strain the decision-making process during a period when time and efficiency is of the essence.

Also, it should be noted that forming and selecting a policy team is the CEO's responsibility. Normally, the policy team would be composed of the top-level executives and special assistants, as needed. To provide flexibility in managing crises, the CEO might elect to call on only those members of the policy team whose expertise is needed for a particular crisis. For example, an organization has a labor dispute; however, the assessment indicates it will have only a moderate impact on the organization. The CEO might then call up the several members of the policy team directly affected by the labor dispute. Thus, we have ensured continued operation of other organizational components and have retained flexibility in our crisis organization.

The policy team initially identifies and clarifies the issues at hand. The team may identify a dozen or so crisis issues. However, after discussion and exchange of views, some issues will be eliminated and some will be compressed into one major issue. It is hoped that many of the policy issues have already been addressed during the planning phase.

The next step: each issue is carefully evaluated for its potential impact. For example, during the early stages of a private carters' strike, the first issue centered on whether city sanitation men should pick up the private refuse. Arguably, such action could facilitate negotiations and prompt the return of the strikers. It would also prevent a severe build-up of the refuse and prevent a possible health emergency. But what if the city sanitation union refused to pick up the refuse? This event might incite the union even more and disrupt negotiations; it could also mean that some residential refuse might be overlooked, thus leading to another health emergency. Finally, if the sanitation union did not pick up the refuse, the commitment of other city resources, such as police and traffic agents, health inspectors, and fire personnel, would be required.

As the sanitation strike scenario demonstrates, each issue of a crisis must be explored in depth and each potential impact carefully evaluated. Having identified, clarified, and evaluated each issue, the team should then formulate its crisis policy. Each element in the policy-formulation process can be seen as a building block upon which the crisis will be managed.

CRISIS LEVELS

Some thought should certainly be given to developing the management policy around the different *crisis levels*. For example, a Level I crisis represents a crisis that would have a significant organization-wide impact. For some organizations, an energy shortage would represent a Level I crisis; however, for others, an energy shortage would not represent a crisis at all. As we can see, the crisis and its impact must be viewed by each organization in the light of its own peculiar social, economic and political environments.

By contrast, a Level II crisis represents an event that would not have organization-wide impact and would not be a significant threat to the survival of the organization. Power failure or a mild earthquake could be considered a Level II situation. Depending on the circumstances, however, an initial Level II could escalate into a Level I. For example, a power failure that initially represents an inconvenience but affects the information system of an organization, could, without a contingency or back up system, escalate into a Level I.

Ordinarily, a Level I incident will be managed under the direction of the chief executive officer. The amount of actual involvement in the management of the event would depend, once again, on the style and personality of the incumbent. However, all CEOs would be involved with the policy team in delineating the policy for managing the crisis.

For the most part, a Level II situation will be managed by the crisis manager, who although responsible for briefing the CEO and keeping him or her informed, will have overall authority to manage the event.

ROLE OF THE CEO

The following two examples show how a public sector CEO managed two labor issues. The first entailed a total strike of public transportation. This strike significantly affected the ability of the municipality to conduct business and provide essential services. In addition, it adversely affected the business community and the general population. This event represented a significant organization-wide impact and required policy direction and management from the CEO.

The second event was a strike by private carters that affected, for the most part, refuse collection in the business community. This can be characterized as an annoyance or interference with business as usual. It did not have significant organizational impact. Furthermore, it did not require the intervention of the CEO. Rather, the crisis team leader managed it quite well, with periodic briefings given to the CEO. This type of management permits the CEO to carry on business with a minimum of organizational interference.

In conclusion, crisis management is a crucial part of organizational life. On an almost daily basis, organizations encounter change—change prompted by the economy, by a competitor, or by an unexpected event. This change—or "turbulence," as Peter Drucker calls it—must be evaluated, planned for, and managed. Organizational survival is the goal of this crisis management program.

1300 P.B